Barbie™

A Year with Barbie

Plan Your Year with Over 35 Tips and Projects

EDDA USA

Always ask a parent or guardian for permission before you try out the delicious recipes and fun crafts found in this book.

Never use knives, scissors, or a stovetop without an adult present.

© 2017 Mattel Inc.

Author: Megan Todd

Layout and cover design: Margret E. Laxness

Drawings on page 34: Lara Gardarsdottir

Printed in India

Distributed by Macmillan

ISBN: 978-1-94078-751-0

www.eddausa.com

TABLE OF CONTENTS

New Year's Diary

Dear Diary,

HAPPY NEW YEAR! I just love saying that. New Year's Day is one of my absolute favorites. It feels great to make a fresh start but also to reflect on the things I learned and tried last year.

My sisters and I were feeling festive and celebrated last night by throwing a New Year's Eve get-together. Stacie decorated the house with purple streamers and silver balloons. It looked sensational! Chelsea and I made a batch of delicious marshmallow treats together. Skipper surprised us all with this amazing edible glitter that she found at our local bakery. We sprinkled it on the marshmallow treats, and they looked fabulous! There's nothing like a little sparkle to ring in the New Year, right?

We spent the rest of the night dancing to great

music (Skipper is such a fantastic DJ!) and sharing our favorite memories from the past year. Like the time last summer when we made homemade soap bubbles that were so big Chelsea thought she could fit inside one. We had so much fun talking about what a great year it was that Stacie started to get bummed that it was over. But that is when I reminded her of all the fun experiences and possibilities that the New Year will bring!

We decided not to make any New Year's resolutions and to just make a promise to ourselves to keep trying new things and make this year even better than the last!

I heard an inspiring quote that I plan on making my words to live by this year: "Nothing is impossible." The word *impossible* itself says, "I'm possible!"

20 ....   ❤ WEEK 1

MONDAY
...... / ......

TUESDAY
...... / ......

WEDNESDAY
...... / ......

THURSDAY
...... / ......

FRIDAY
...... / ......

SATURDAY
...... / ......

SUNDAY
...... / ......

MONDAY
.... / ....

TUESDAY
.... / ....

WEDNESDAY
.... / ....

THURSDAY
.... / ....

FRIDAY
.... / ....

SATURDAY
.... / ....

SUNDAY
.... / ....

MY DREAMS

If you can dream it, you can do it.
Do you want to be the first person on Mars,
a musician, or maybe a deep-sea explorer?
Write down your dreams here.

DREAMS

Wow, when you dream, you dream **BIG!**
What do you do next?

Set goals! Goals are smaller dreams that you can easily achieve. So before you can be a rockstar, you can say, "I want to learn how to play [my favorite song]."

GOALS

Now, think about all of the **small steps** you can take to achieve those goals. For example, "Practice the guitar every day for 30 minutes."

STEPS

Now you've got it!
What will you dream next?

20........ ❤ WEEK 3

MONDAY
...... / ......

TUESDAY
...... / ......

WEDNESDAY
...... / ......

THURSDAY
...... / ......

FRIDAY
...... / ......

SATURDAY
...... / ......

SUNDAY
...... / ......

MONDAY
...... / ......

TUESDAY
...... / ......

WEDNESDAY
...... / ......

THURSDAY
...... / ......

FRIDAY
...... / ......

SATURDAY
...... / ......

SUNDAY
...... / ......

"HI!
I've been thinking a lot lately about confidence.
Sometimes even the little things, like raising your hand
in class to answer a question, can seem difficult. Here are
some of the things that help inspire me to speak up and
stand out!"

– BARBIE

Don't compare yourself to others. Everyone is doing
and learning things in their own time. Focus on being
the best **YOU** you can be.

Write down the things that **make you awesome.**
Being confident is all about knowing who you really are.
Always remind yourself of the things that make
you positively you.

**Stand up for what you know
is right.** Write down some of the
things that are **important to you.**
This is what raising your voice is all
about!

When trying new things, ask yourself:
"what's the worst that could happen?"
Usually, when we think long and hard about doing
things that are out of our comfort zone, we realize
that the worst-case scenario isn't actually that
bad.

MONDAY
.... / ....

TUESDAY
.... / ....

WEDNESDAY
.... / ....

THURSDAY
.... / ....

FRIDAY
.... / ....

SATURDAY
.... / ....

SUNDAY
.... / ....

POETRY is a beautiful way to express yourself. Fill in the blanks to make a unique poem that allows your voice to be heard!

I AM .... AND ....
(two special things about you)

I HOPE ....
(something that you hope for)

I HEAR ....
(a sound that you love)

I AM .... AND ....
(first line of the poem repeated)

I DREAM ....
(something that you dream about)

I SEE ....
(something that you love to see)

I SAY ....
(something you believe in)

I AM .... AND ....
(first line of the poem repeated)

MONDAY
.... / ....

TUESDAY
.... / ....

WEDNESDAY
.... / ....

THURSDAY
.... / ....

FRIDAY
.... / ....

SATURDAY
.... / ....

SUNDAY
.... / ....

Sparkle Beads Valentine

This year, Barbie and her sisters are going to make Valentines for all of their friends. These beaded hearts are fun to make, and they have just the right amount of sparkle and shine!

What You'll Need

Red cardstock ❤ Parchment paper ❤ Scissors Craft glue ❤ Paintbrush Seed beads (red, pink, and gold, mixed together, look great!)

The Steps

1. Trace and cut a heart shape that's six inches at its widest part out of the cardstock!

2. Write your Valentine message on one side of the heart. A couple of ideas you could try: **"Shine on, Valentine"** or, **"I love your sparkle!"**

3. Turn the heart over and lay it on the parchment paper.

4. On the blank side of the heart, spread a layer of glue over the entire heart with the paintbrush. Don't worry about making it too even – the thicker spots will grab more beads.

5. Sprinkle the seed beads onto the glue in a thick layer. Let dry.

♥ WEEK 7   20 ....

MONDAY

...... / ......

TUESDAY

...... / ......

WEDNESDAY

...... / ......

THURSDAY

...... / ......

FRIDAY

...... / ......

SATURDAY

...... / ......

SUNDAY

...... / ......

BE YOU!

Every single thing about you – big and small – is what makes you unique!

Birthday

_____

Age

_____

Draw a
self-portrait
here

FAVORITES

Food

Color

_____

_____

Book

Game

_____

_____

Movie

_____

HOBBIES

_____

_____

_____

_____

_____

_____

_____

_____

20........   ♥ WEEK 8

MONDAY
...... / ......

TUESDAY
...... / ......

WEDNESDAY
...... / ......

THURSDAY
...... / ......

FRIDAY
...... / ......

SATURDAY
...... / ......

SUNDAY
...... / ......

20 ....

MONDAY

.... / ....

TUESDAY

.... / ....

WEDNESDAY

.... / ....

THURSDAY

.... / ....

FRIDAY

.... / ....

SATURDAY

.... / ....

SUNDAY

.... / ....

Birthday Diary

DEAR DIARY,

Today is my BIRTHDAY! I think it may have been my best ever. My friends and family threw me a surprise party! Well, that is, they tried to throw a surprise party. Chelsea sort of spilled the beans, when I overheard her talking about cupcakes! I didn't let them know I was on to them, though.

It's definitely safe to say that my family and friends know me well, because get this: It was a make-your-own-pizza party! Our kitchen was transformed into a retro pizza parlor. Everyone wore matching aprons and giant, white chef hats. There

22

were so many toppings to choose from: pepperoni, mushrooms, pineapple, and even anchovies! (No thank you!)

We had such a great time making the pizzas together. I made mine heart shaped and LOADED it with cheese! Stacie was feeling bold and tried to throw her dough into the air like a pizza maker. She was great at the tossing, but not so good at the catching!

I took my birthday wish pretty seriously this year. I thought long and hard about what I would do when it was time to blow out the candles. I have SO MANY wishes, it was hard to pick just one! I closed my eyes, took a deep breath, and said to myself, "I wish to make this my best year ever." I want to keep exploring, discovering, and trying new things. Every. Single. Day!

Do you have a special birthday wish this year? Write it down here!

....

....

....

....

20......... 🖤 WEEK 10

MONDAY
.... / ....

TUESDAY
.... / ....

WEDNESDAY
.... / ....

THURSDAY
.... / ....

FRIDAY
.... / ....

SATURDAY
.... / ....

SUNDAY
.... / ....

❤ WEEK 11   20 ....

MONDAY

.... / ....

TUESDAY

.... / ....

WEDNESDAY

.... / ....

THURSDAY

.... / ....

FRIDAY

.... / ....

SATURDAY

.... / ....

SUNDAY

.... / ....

Friendship Flowers

I love my friends. They each have qualities that make them unique and special. Friends are the flowers in the garden of life! They make our world more colorful and so much fun. Who are some of your friends and what qualities do they have that make your life better?

♥ **WEEK 12**   20 ....

MONDAY
...... / ......

TUESDAY
...... / ......

WEDNESDAY
...... / ......

THURSDAY
...... / ......

FRIDAY
...... / ......

SATURDAY
...... / ......

SUNDAY
...... / ......

Chelsea's Strawberry Cupcakes

If there's one thing that Chelsea knows, it's cupcakes! What better way to welcome spring than with these scrumptious and perfectly pink strawberry cupcakes?

What You'll Need

For the cupcakes
- 2 cups self-rising flour
- 1¼ cup fine sugar
- 2 sticks softened, unsalted butter
- 4 large eggs
- 1 teaspoon vanilla extract
- 4 tablespoons milk
- Paper baking cups
- Cupcake pan
- Electric mixer

For the strawberry buttercream frosting
- 2 sticks softened, unsalted butter
- 1 cup powdered sugar
- 1 cup strawberry preserves
- Pinch of salt

The Steps

1. Preheat oven to 400°F. Line a cupcake pan with paper baking cups.
2. In an electric mixer, mix the sugar and butter. Now add the eggs, vanilla, and milk, and mix well. Finally, add in the flour, one cup at a time, mixing well after each cup.
3. Spoon batter into cupcake pan. Bake for 15-20 minutes.
4. With the electric mixer, cream the butter and sugar at medium speed. Add the strawberry preserves and mix well. Frost the cupcakes after they have cooled.

MONDAY

.... / ....

TUESDAY

.... / ....

WEDNESDAY

.... / ....

THURSDAY

.... / ....

FRIDAY

.... / ....

SATURDAY

.... / ....

SUNDAY

.... / ....

HAIRSTYLE PERSONALITY QUIZ

Which hairstyle fits your personality the best?
Take this quiz to find out!

1. Time for an impromptu dance party! What song are you going to play?

A Pop please: Anything with a great beat that can get me moving.

B A song with great lyrics. I love to sing AND dance!

C Classical! I love practicing ballet techniques.

D Anything that rocks: Like me!

2. Which of these careers sound interesting?

A Chef **B** Veterinarian **C** Pilot **D** Teacher

3. Time to get your grub on! What sounds best to you?

A A berry smoothie, or anything that gives me energy!

B A sandwich. I like things I can eat while reading or studying.

C A big family dinner, I love sharing food AND laughter!

D Lemon meringue tarts or strawberry cupcakes, I love anything that is sweet!

4. Pick your dream vacation:

A Hiking in the mountains.

B A weekend at my favorite amusement park.

C Beach fun.

D Exploring a new city.

5. It's picture day! Choose an outfit that expresses you best.

A A cute dress with just the right necklace, of course!

B A long-sleeved shirt in my favorite color.

C A tank top with a cardigan. I love layers!

D A trendy tee that expresses who I am!

Scoring:

1. A-2, B-1, C-0, D-3   2. A-3, B-2, C-0, D-3   3. A-2, B-0, C-1, D-3

4. A-2, B-3, C-1, D-0   5. A-0, B-1, C-2, D-3

0 - 4 points: Shoulder-length and natural. You're determined and a free thinker. You're great at solving problems, and you're always the first person your friends turn to for help.

4 - 8 points: Long and wavy. You are kind and a great friend. You aren't afraid to put in extra effort, and you always try your best.

8 - 12 points: Sporty bob. You're always on the go and love being active. Everyone knows that if you're around, they're sure to have a great time.

12 points or more: Ponytail with bangs. You're chic and fashion-forward. You know exactly what it takes to be fabulously you. Your friends always look to you for the latest style trends.

20 .... ♥ WEEK 14

MONDAY
.... / ....

TUESDAY
.... / ....

WEDNESDAY
.... / ....

THURSDAY
.... / ....

FRIDAY
.... / ....

SATURDAY
.... / ....

SUNDAY
.... / ....

MONDAY
...... / ......

TUESDAY
...... / ......

WEDNESDAY
...... / ......

THURSDAY
...... / ......

FRIDAY
...... / ......

SATURDAY
...... / ......

SUNDAY
...... / ......

ORIGAMI ENVELOPE

Add a fun twist to the notes that you send your friends by using the Japanese art of origami to fold them into their own envelopes.

1. Begin by writing your note on a piece of paper (8.5-by-11 inches).

2. With the paper on its side (so the shorter sides are on the left and right), and the writing facing upwards, fold it in half, and then unfold. The line that you just made is called the center crease.

3. Fold the left and right sides to the center crease and unfold. This is called the cupboard crease, because it looks like two doors that can open and close.

4. Fold the top corners down to the center crease, like if you were making a paper airplane.

5. Refold the cupboard crease that you made in step 3 (bottom left and right sides to the center crease). Don't unfold.

6. Fold the top point down to the triangular space that fits it, and then unfold.

7. From the center, expand the diamond-shaped pocket on the crease you made in step 6 and flatten out to the sides.

8. Fold the bottom left and right corners to the center crease, making a triangle out of the bottom section, below the flattened portion from step 7.

9. Insert the triangle into the pocket that you've made.

10. On the other side, you can address your letter to whomever you're sending it to!

2.
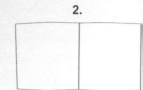

4.
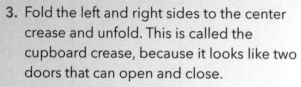

5.
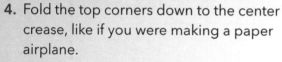

7.
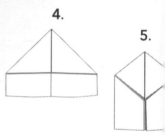

8.
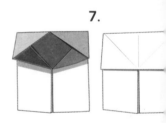

9.
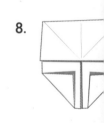

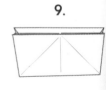

MONDAY

...... / ......

TUESDAY

...... / ......

WEDNESDAY

...... / ......

THURSDAY

...... / ......

FRIDAY

...... / ......

SATURDAY

...... / ......

SUNDAY

...... / ......

WHAT HAPPENS NEXT?

**What happens next?
Create your very own Barbie story here.**

It was a beautiful spring morning and the cheerful sound of birds chirping filled the crisp air. Barbie and her sisters were gathered together in their backyard.

"I'm so excited!" Chelsea said in her usual upbeat voice.

"I don't think we've ever tackled a project THIS big before!" Stacie agreed.

"One thing is for sure: we'll certainly have our hands full this weekend."

"But I know we can do it!" Barbie added.

"Well, what are we waiting for? Let's get started!" Skipper exclaimed as she excitedly picked up a …

20........   ❤ WEEK 17

MONDAY
.... / ....

TUESDAY
.... / ....

WEDNESDAY
.... / ....

THURSDAY
.... / ....

FRIDAY
.... / ....

SATURDAY
.... / ....

SUNDAY
.... / ....

MONDAY
.... / ....

TUESDAY
.... / ....

WEDNESDAY
.... / ....

THURSDAY
.... / ....

FRIDAY
.... / ....

SATURDAY
.... / ....

SUNDAY
.... / ....

Friendship Bouquets

What better way to welcome the wonderful month of May than by making little flower bouquets for all of your friends? These paper cones are traditionally left on the doors of friends on the first day of May, but they also look super cute hanging from desk chairs or lockers!

What You'll Need

- Small bouquet of flowers
- 1 sheet of decorative paper
- Double-stick tape
- Thin string
- Hole-punch
- Paper towel
- Plastic sandwich bag

The Steps

1. Roll the decorative paper into a cone shape.
2. Secure the cone with double-stick tape, placed at the seam.
3. Hold the cone, pointy-side down, and punch two holes on either side, about 1-2 inches from the top of the cone.
4. Cut a 12-inch length of string. Thread it through the holes and tie knots to secure. Trim off excess string.
5. Wrap the stems of the bouquet with a very moist paper towel and place into the sandwich bag. Place the bouquet into the cone. Make sure to tuck the plastic bag out of view.

❤ Week 19

20 ....

Monday

.... / ....

Tuesday

.... / ....

Wednesday

.... / ....

Thursday

.... / ....

Friday

.... / ....

Saturday

.... / ....

Sunday

.... / ....

DREAMHOUSE

What Would Be in Your Dreamhouse?

Barbie's Dreamhouse is a place where Barbie and her sisters can dream big and imagine that anything is possible.

Let your imagination soar and think about all the fun
things that would be in **your dreamhouse!** Would your
dreamhouse have an automatic
hot chocolate machine?
Or maybe an enormous coral reef aquarium?

Get creative:

20........ ♥ WEEK 20

MONDAY
.... / ....

TUESDAY
.... / ....

WEDNESDAY
.... / ....

THURSDAY
.... / ....

FRIDAY
.... / ....

SATURDAY
.... / ....

SUNDAY
.... / ....

♥ WEEK 21   20 ....

MONDAY

...... / ......

TUESDAY

...... / ......

WEDNESDAY

.... / ....

THURSDAY

...... / ....

FRIDAY

.... / ....

SATURDAY

...... / ......

SUNDAY

.... / ....

WHICH CHARACTER ARE YOU?

Are you always up for trying new things like Barbie? Are your afternoons positively packed with activities like Stacie? Or are you curious and imaginative like Chelsea? Take this quiz to see who you have the most in common with!

1. Your best friend has a BIG problem. How do you help her through it?

A A nice long talk while drinking hot chocolate and marshmallows can help solve ANY problem.

B A dance party! Music helps everything!

C By taking a hike together. The fresh air can really clear your head.

D I'd do something nice for her to lift her spirits, like bringing her flowers or writing a thoughtful note.

2. The school is putting on a play! Are you going to try out?

A Absolutely, I love performing!

B Yes, I love dressing up in costumes!

C Nah, I prefer to run things behind the scenes.

D Sure, I love trying new things!

3. You've found yourself with some free time on a Saturday evening. How do you want to spend it?

A Learn how to knit a scarf. I love trying and making new things!

B I'm going to take hundreds of selfies and edit them with the craziest filters I can.

C I feel like shooting hoops with some friends.

D A new coffee shop opened in my neighborhood. I'm going to grab my bestie and get a couple of caramel mochas!

4. You're helping out in the community garden this afternoon. Which flowers do you want to plant first?
A Zinnias. Not only do they look cool, but their name is fun to say!
B Sunflowers. They're cheerful and bold, just like me!
C Roses. I just love classics and they smell SO amazing.
D Daisies. I love that they're so energetic that they bloom twice a year!

5. Time to chill out and take it easy! Which activity helps you relax the most?
A Listening to my favorite songs.
B Yoga and stretching are my favorite ways to relax.
C Origami! Folding and looking at colorful paper is so calming.
D Curling up with a great book.

Scoring:
1. A-0, B-1, C-2, D-3 2. A-3, B-0, C-2, D-1 3. A-0, B-2, C-3, D-1
4. A-2, B-1, C-0, D-3 5. A-2, B-3, C-0, D-1

0 - 4 points. You're most like Barbie! You're friendly and know exactly who you are and what you like. You love trying new things and staying curious.

4 - 8 points: You're Chelsea! You're cheerful and spontaneous. You have a great imagination and are always eager to lend a helping hand!

8 - 12 points: You're Skipper! You're a wiz at technology and love being creative!

12 points or more: You're Stacie! You're energetic and everyone loves your company. You're active and tackle any challenge with enthusiasm.

Picture Taking Tips

Skipper knows a thing or two when it comes to snapping the best pics! With the school year coming to an end, it's a great time to take photos of you and your friends. Here are Skipper's top tricks to getting the best shots possible. Having fun while capturing your marvelous moments is what it's all about!

1. Be yourself. Whether you go for a silly face or a dazzling smile, if you're being yourself, no photo can look bad!

2. Find fun angles. Taking photos from different angles can make your photos more interesting. Try placing your camera in different positions, creating different angles to find your favorite!

3. Background. Use interesting backgrounds to tell a story with your photo. At the movies with your friends? Try to get the marquee in the shot.

4. Filtered. Take your original pictures with the normal lens and add the filters later. This gives you a chance to be creative and try a lot of different versions!

MONDAY
...... / ......

TUESDAY
...... / ......

WEDNESDAY
...... / ......

THURSDAY
...... / ......

FRIDAY
...... / ......

SATURDAY
...... / ......

SUNDAY
...... / ......

Summer Fun Checklist

Here is Barbie's *ultimate* summer fun checklist. See how many you can cross off to make this summer your most memorable one yet!

- ☐ Backyard campout
- ☐ Water balloon fight
- ☐ Climb a tree
- ☐ Splash in summer rain puddles
- ☐ Learn how to say "hello" in three different languages
- ☐ Read a book outside
- ☐ Go on a hike
- ☐ Stay up super late
- ☐ Watch fireworks
- ☐ Bake something delicious
- ☐ Choreograph a dance to your favorite summer song
- ☐ Write a letter to a friend
- ☐ Fly a kite
- ☐ Visit the library
- ☐ Watch a sunset
- ☐ Make a pitcher of lemonade
- ☐ Watch a movie outdoors
- ☐ Make a collage from images that inspire you
- ☐ Make friendship bracelets

MONDAY
.... / ....

TUESDAY
.... / ....

WEDNESDAY
.... / ....

THURSDAY
.... / ....

FRIDAY
.... / ....

SATURDAY
.... / ....

SUNDAY
.... / ....

Camping Trip Diary

☆ **MOOD:** Happy

Dear Diary,

It's the first week of June and that can only mean one thing: It's time for the annual family camping trip! It really is one of my favorite things about summer. I love everything about it. Even getting there is fun. The road trip has such beautiful scenery, and Skipper makes a perfect playlist filled with all of our favorite songs that we sing along to.

I'm not sure which tradition is my favorite. Pitching our big blue tent together, telling stories while roasting marshmallows, or stargazing with my sisters. Or maybe it's just spending time outdoors! This year didn't quite go as usual, though. The great outdoors had a pretty big surprise in store for us.

Rain. So. Much. Rain.

I mean, don't get me wrong, I like a good rainy day just as much as the next girl. But while camping? Not so much.

We had to quickly gather up our supplies and take shelter in the tent for the night.

But you know what? We still ended up having a great time! We had a flashlight dance party, told stories, and sang our favorite songs. We also discovered that marshmallows are just as delicious right out of the bag as they are roasted! Even though things didn't turn out like they usually do, we still ended up making great memories and spending time together, which is what a family vacation is all about!

20........ ❤ WEEK 24

MONDAY
...... / ......

TUESDAY
...... / ......

WEDNESDAY
...... / ......

THURSDAY
...... / ......

FRIDAY
...... / ......

SATURDAY
...... / ......

SUNDAY
...... / ......

♥ WEEK 25   20 ....

MONDAY

.... / ....

TUESDAY

.... / ....

WEDNESDAY

.... / ....

THURSDAY

.... / ....

FRIDAY

.... / ....

SATURDAY

.... / ....

SUNDAY

.... / ....

MARSHMALLOW ROASTING STICKS

Pass the s'mores!
Make these little marshmallow-roasting sticks
for all of your Barbie dolls!

WHAT YOU'LL NEED

Wood toothpicks • Cotton ball • Scissors
Craft glue (white or clear) • Small rubber bands or string

THE STEPS

1. If you're using a toothpick that's pointed on both ends, cut off one pointy end with scissors.
2. Unravel a cotton ball and tear off a small piece that is 1 inch in length and half an inch wide.
3. Using your fingers, spread a small amount of craft glue onto one side of the cotton.
4. Place the pointy side of the toothpick at one end of the piece of cotton and roll the cotton around the toothpick to make a marshmallow shape. Let dry.
5. Attach to the doll's hands with a small rubber band or string.

MONDAY

.... / ....

TUESDAY

.... / ....

WEDNESDAY

.... / ....

THURSDAY

.... / ....

FRIDAY

.... / ....

SATURDAY

.... / ....

SUNDAY

.... / ....

CONSTELLATION DOT-TO-DOT

Stargazing is one of Barbie's favorite things to do in the summer. There's just something about looking up at the stars that makes the impossible seem possible!

Complete these constellation dot-to-dots and see if you can spot them in the night sky!

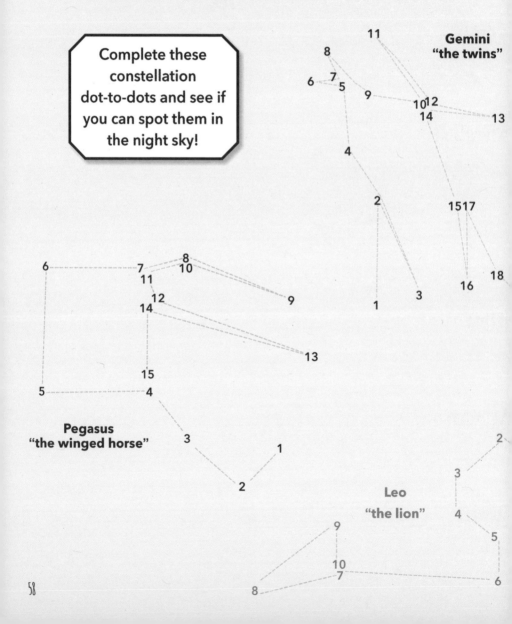

Gemini
"the twins"

Pegasus
"the winged horse"

Leo
"the lion"

❤ WEEK 27   20 ....

MONDAY

.... / ....

TUESDAY

.... / ....

WEDNESDAY

.... / ....

THURSDAY

.... / ....

FRIDAY

.... / ....

SATURDAY

.... / ....

SUNDAY

.... / ....

Barbie's Summer Memory Jar

"I'VE HAD SUCH A GREAT SUMMER and have made so many great memories with my sisters! I never want to forget playing water balloon games with Stacie, watching the funniest movie I've ever seen with Skipper, and making sand castles in the backyard with Chelsea. That's why this year I'm making a Summer Memory Jar! It's filled with all sorts of mementos like sand and a movie ticket stub and it also looks cool on my bookshelf!"

— BARBIE

What You'll Need

- A clean glass jar with lid
- Small objects from your summer
- Masking tape
- Marker

Steps

All summer long, collect items to put in your memory jar. Be on the lookout for things like seashells, rocks, sand, glitter, flower petals, ticket stubs, bottle caps, and ribbon. You can even write down a special memory on a small piece of paper! No matter which items you choose, you're sure to have your own special, one of a kind jar of memories.

When you're finished filling your jar, use the masking tape to label the outside of the jar with your name and the year.

20........ ❤ WEEK 28

MONDAY
.... / ....

TUESDAY
.... / ....

WEDNESDAY
.... / ....

THURSDAY
.... / ....

FRIDAY
.... / ....

SATURDAY
.... / ....

SUNDAY
.... / ....

♥ WEEK 29   20 ....

MONDAY

...... / ......

TUESDAY

...... / ......

WEDNESDAY

...... / ......

THURSDAY

...... / ......

FRIDAY

...... / ......

SATURDAY

...... / ......

SUNDAY

...... / ......

Getting Active with Barbie

Yoga is one of Barbie's favorite ways to start her day. Follow these steps for a full body stretch that will make you feel ready for anything! Take off your shoes, grab a towel and let's get moving!

Welcome the sun: Stand straight with your arms at your side. Facing forward take three deep breaths and slowly bring both arms above your head, bringing your palms together. Hold for three breaths and then repeat.

Standing forward bend: Stand straight with your arms at your side. Facing forward, take three deep breaths. Moving slowly, bend your upper body at the hips, bringing your nose in line with your knees. Stop when you feel too much resistance. Hold for three deep breaths.

Tree Pose: This yoga stretch also helps sharpen your brain by making you focus on your balance. Slowly bring one leg up, placing your foot on your inner thigh. Hold for three breaths, slowly lower your leg and then repeat with your other leg.

Warrior: Standing straight, take three deep breaths and move your right leg in front. Slowly bend your right knee, keeping your left leg straight. Slowly extend your arms, with your right one facing forwards and your left one behind you. Hold for three breaths, then straighten your right leg and bring it back to standing position. Repeat sequence with your left leg.

❤ WEEK 30   20 ....

MONDAY
.... / ....

TUESDAY
.... / ....

WEDNESDAY
.... / ....

THURSDAY
.... / ....

FRIDAY
.... / ....

SATURDAY
.... / ....

SUNDAY
.... / ....

65

Water Balloon Games

Beat the summer heat by playing these outdoor water balloon games. Be prepared to get wet!

What You'll Need

- Water balloons
- 2 buckets
- 2 laundry baskets
- Music
- Timer

Hot Balloon

Put on some music, stand in a circle, and take turns throwing a water balloon to the player next to you. If you throw it to someone and they don't catch it (or it pops) that person is out. If the music stops playing and you're holding the balloon, you've got the Hot Balloon!

Pop and Dash

Set out two buckets and place laundry baskets full of balloons next to them. Split into two teams, each team lining up 10 feet behind the buckets. Set the timer for 2 minutes and let the two players at the front of the lines grab a balloon and pop it over the bucket. Once popped, the player must high-five the next player in line, signaling their turn. When the time is up, the team with the most water in their bucket wins!

❤ WEEK 31   20 ....

MONDAY

...... / ......

TUESDAY

...... / ......

WEDNESDAY

.... / ......

THURSDAY

.... / ......

FRIDAY

.... / ......

SATURDAY

...... / ......

SUNDAY

.... / ......

Ribbon Headband Craft

This totally chic ribbon headband is a breeze to make. The best part is that you can choose the color and style to make it completely you.

What You'll Need

- Scissors
- A flexible tape measure
- Ribbon (Pick a decorative ribbon that matches your style. Think velvet, satin, or patterned, but no wider than 2 inches.)
- Sewing needle
- Thread that closely matches the ribbon color
- Elastic

The Steps

1. Around your head, where you'll be wearing your headband, use the tape measure to determine the length of ribbon you'll need.
2. Cut the ribbon 1½ inches shorter than your measurement. Cut a 2-inch piece of elastic.
3. Fold one end of the ribbon lengthwise over one end of the elastic. Be sure that the tail of your elastic is away from the ribbon.
4. With the needle and thread, make several stitches back and forth at the end of the ribbon and through the elastic. Measure the headband where you'll wear it on your head again to see if any elastic needs to be trimmed. Repeat for the other end of the ribbon.

♥ WEEK 32   20........

MONDAY
.... / ....

TUESDAY
.... / ....

WEDNESDAY
.... / ....

THURSDAY
.... / ....

FRIDAY
.... / ....

SATURDAY
.... / ....

SUNDAY
.... / ....

69

WORD SEARCH

Oh no! Barbie and the gang's pets have gone missing! Can you help find them? Look for words across, down, backward, and diagonally.

DJ • Honey • Rookie • Taffy • Tawny • Blissa • Sequin • Lacey • Ruff • Sutton • Rugby • Scrunchie • Hudson

A	W	C	I	Y	O	K	E	E	X	O	H	O	B	R
G	L	Y	F	S	H	O	N	E	Y	Q	K	L	Q	F
U	O	F	S	U	D	N	I	Q	P	X	I	L	I	H
U	A	Z	G	T	M	K	L	Y	W	S	X	N	P	X
T	B	X	K	T	O	M	H	N	S	S	I	V	L	D
F	Z	L	T	O	O	J	J	A	P	E	N	I	D	T
U	G	A	R	N	C	D	M	E	W	Q	X	S	B	D
B	V	C	Q	M	U	S	E	Y	W	U	V	M	G	L
H	Q	E	S	C	G	E	I	F	X	I	L	H	Z	O
H	U	Y	L	K	K	E	I	H	C	N	U	R	C	S
L	W	D	N	X	P	K	B	R	U	G	B	Y	W	I
C	V	E	S	W	P	R	Q	E	B	L	X	W	F	P
H	M	M	R	O	A	E	R	Z	T	V	M	X	D	Y
E	L	S	P	E	N	T	I	T	B	Y	I	X	I	K
Z	V	M	E	B	D	P	Z	F	F	U	R	Q	F	G

♥ WEEK 33   20 ....

MONDAY
...... / ......

TUESDAY
...... / ......

WEDNESDAY
...... / ......

THURSDAY
...... / ......

FRIDAY
...... / ......

SATURDAY
...... / ......

SUNDAY
...... / ......

71

STACIE'S TRIPLE BERRY SMOOTHIE

If you are anything like Stacie, you've been pretty active this summer! Cool off with this awesome Triple Berry Smoothie. Stacie's special trick to making the smoothies extra yummy: use frozen berries instead of ice!

WHAT YOU'LL NEED

Makes two

- ⅓ cup frozen strawberries
- ⅓ cup frozen raspberries
- ⅓ cup frozen blueberries
- 1 frozen banana
- ½ cup orange juice
- ½ cup milk
- Blender

Place ingredients into the blender in the order listed. Blend until nice and smooth.

20.........

MONDAY

...... / ......

TUESDAY

...... / ......

WEDNESDAY

...... / ......

THURSDAY

...... / ......

FRIDAY

...... / ......

SATURDAY

...... / ......

SUNDAY

...... / ......

CREATE YOUR PERFECT PLAYLIST

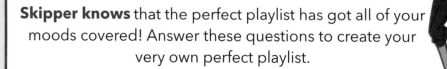

Skipper knows that the perfect playlist has got all of your moods covered! Answer these questions to create your very own perfect playlist.

What song makes you instantly happy? ....

What is your favorite song to dance to?.....................................

What is your favorite song to sing along with? ....

What is your favorite jam to listen to in the car?...................................

What song inspires you?...

When you need to focus, what tune do you play? ....

What track sounds best on your headphones?.................................

What song makes you feel energized and ready to go?

....

What is your favorite song to put on when you're cleaning your

room? ....

Which is the best tune to play while hanging out with friends?

....

What song makes you feel creative?...

What is your favorite song to chill out to?.................................

Now you have created your perfect playlist!
Share it with your friends!

♥ **WEEK 35**   20 ....

MONDAY
.... / ....

TUESDAY
.... / ....

WEDNESDAY
.... / ....

THURSDAY
.... / ....

FRIDAY
.... / ....

SATURDAY
.... / ....

SUNDAY
.... / ....

75

Back to School Diary

MOOD: Excited!

Dear Diary,

Summer has officially come to an end. I will miss the long warm days, that's for sure.

Tomorrow is the first day of school! I am so excited to get back to see all of my friends after the break. I'm a little nervous, though, about starting a new grade. I wonder what it will be like.

I had a lot of fun choosing the ultimate back-to-school outfit. I decided on comfy jeans and the cutest purple T-shirt! It has a big picture of a puppy wearing sunglasses on the front that looks JUST like Honey!

Yesterday I told Stacie that the most important thing a person can wear is their confidence! Isn't that the truth! I'll be sure to remember to put that on in the morning, too!

♥ WEEK 36   20 ....

MONDAY
.... / ....

TUESDAY
.... / ....

WEDNESDAY
.... / ....

THURSDAY
.... / ....

FRIDAY
.... / ....

SATURDAY
.... / ....

SUNDAY
.... / ....

PERSONAL STYLE

For each pair of words, circle the one that you think describes you better. Then add them to your **My Style** list. If you feel like they *both* describe you, just add both—there are no rules! When you're finished, you'll have a personal style list that is totally and uniquely you.

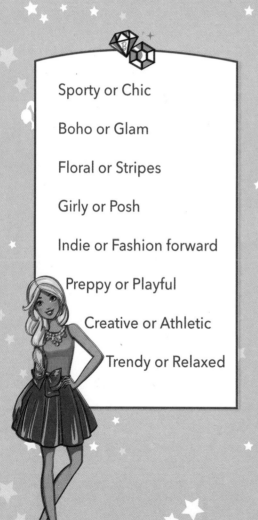

Sporty or Chic

Boho or Glam

Floral or Stripes

Girly or Posh

Indie or Fashion forward

Preppy or Playful

Creative or Athletic

Trendy or Relaxed

❤ WEEK 37   20 ....

MONDAY
...... / ....

TUESDAY
...... / ....

WEDNESDAY
.... / ....

THURSDAY
.... / ....

FRIDAY
.... / ....

SATURDAY
...... / ....

SUNDAY
...... / ....

Homemade Beauty Masks

"**There is nothing** better than a girl's night with my sisters! We love making silly videos, dancing, and spending time together. During one of my very favorite girl's nights we made these amazing facial masks out of natural ingredients. Grab **YOUR** best girls and give them a try!"

Barbie's Oatmeal and Honey Mask
This mask is gentle and calming. The oatmeal soothes while the honey is *super* cleansing. In a mixing bowl, stir to combine one tablespoon of oatmeal and one tablespoon of honey. Apply to cheeks, chin, and forehead. After 15 minutes, remove the mask with warm water and a washcloth.

Stacie's Simple Egg White Mask
Egg whites are packed with vitamins and minerals that are wonderful for your skin. Simply separate the yolk from the white and apply the whites of the egg to your face with a brush. Leave on until dry. Remove the mask with warm water and a washcloth.

Skipper's Creamy Avocado Mask
Avocado is intensely moisturizing and loaded with vitamin E (which is great for your skin). Cut an avocado in half and remove the pit. Mash the avocado with a fork in a bowl and apply to your face, leaving it on for 10-15 minutes. Remove the mask with warm water and a washcloth.

MONDAY
.... / ....

TUESDAY
.... / ....

WEDNESDAY
.... / ....

THURSDAY
.... / ....

FRIDAY
.... / ....

SATURDAY
.... / ....

SUNDAY
.... / ....

WHAT DO YOU WANT TO BE?

You can be anything. A surgeon, a dancer, a scientist,
or a computer game programmer! And the best part?
You don't even have to choose just ONE thing to be.
Not only can you be *anything*,
you can be MANY things!

Write down some of the things you dream of being.
Remember: If you can dream it, you can do it!

♥ **WEEK 39**   20 ....

MONDAY
...... / ......

TUESDAY
...... / ......

WEDNESDAY
...... / ......

THURSDAY
...... / ......

FRIDAY
...... / ......

SATURDAY
...... / ......

SUNDAY
...... / ......

Best Friends

What would we do without our best friends? They're always there when we need someone to lean on. They're *full* of great advice, just when you need it the most. And not to mention, they're SO MUCH fun to be around! Grab your best friend and fill out this fun page together!

My best friend is ....

She is my best friend because ....

We met at ....

Her birthday is .... Her dream is to be a ....

Her favorite color is ....

Her star sign is .... Her motto is ....

My best friend is happiest when ....

Some of our favorite things to do together are ....

.... and of course, ...

Some of the most important things we have in common:

....

....

We also appreciate our differences. For example, she prefers

.... but I prefer ....

My best friend can always make me laugh by ....

....

Our favorite movie to watch together is ....

We quote it *constantly*!

Some of our favorite songs to sing together are ....

....

Our dream is to one day go to ....

together.

♥ WEEK 40   20........

MONDAY

...... / ......

TUESDAY

...... / ......

WEDNESDAY

...... / ......

THURSDAY

...... / ......

FRIDAY

...... / ......

SATURDAY

...... / ......

SUNDAY

...... / ......

Helping Others

Giving back is an important step to becoming the best *you* that you can be. There are so many ways to help others, and even small gestures can have a **BIG** impact. Try one of these acts of kindness to brighten someone's day.

- ❤ Bake cookies for a neighbor
- ❤ Write an inspiring note for someone
- ❤ Collect food for a local food bank
- ❤ Start a crafting club at a nursing home
- ❤ Offer to tutor a friend in a subject they're having trouble with
- ❤ Wash a car
- ❤ Volunteer at an animal shelter
- ❤ Give a compliment
- ❤ Offer to read someone a story
- ❤ Donate old clothes

♥ WEEK 41   20 ....

MONDAY
.... / ....

TUESDAY
.... / ....

WEDNESDAY
.... / ....

THURSDAY
.... / ....

FRIDAY
.... / ....

SATURDAY
.... / ....

SUNDAY
.... / ....

Halloween Story

Get into the Halloween spirit by writing your very own spooktacular Barbie Halloween story.
Choose two characters, one plot, and one place and see where your story goes!

Characters: Barbie • Stacie • Skipper • Chelsea • Nikki • Theresa • Summer
Plot: Plan a spooky celebration • Solve a mystery • Help a friend in need • Find an unusual object
Place: Home • The forest • Pumpkin patch • School

Story

.... and .... in/at ....
(Character)   (Character)   (Plot)   (Place)

....

....

....

....

....

....

....

MONDAY

.... / ....

TUESDAY

.... / ....

WEDNESDAY

.... / ....

THURSDAY

.... / ....

FRIDAY

.... / ....

SATURDAY

.... / ....

SUNDAY

.... / ....

HALLOWEEN DIARY

☆ MOOD: Inspired

DEAR DIARY,

I have to say that this was one spooktacular Halloween! It was full of our usual family traditions. We went trick-or treating in our neighborhood. I think it was a record year for candy!

Afterwards we always end the evening by watching our favorite Halloween movie and staying up late telling each other spooky stories.

This year we also started a new tradition. My sisters and I challenged ourselves to create our Halloween costumes using clothing and accessories that we already had, rather than buying new ones!

Everyone had such a great time getting creative with costume ideas. Chelsea was an adorable black kitten. She found a black leotard and leggings and glued black triangles to a headband and painted whiskers on her cheeks. Stacie was a cowgirl. She found a cowboy hat and wore it with jeans and boots. Skipper outdid herself by making an AMAZING jellyfish costume using an old umbrella and streamers! She is so clever!

And me? I decided to recycle the tutu I wore in last year's ballet recital of Swan Lake. I glued faux flowers all over my ballet costume and made a wand with a chopstick, some glitter, and even more flowers. It was a pretty good flower fairy transformation if I do say so myself!

It was such a fun challenge, and being creative made our Halloween even more special. I'm already brainstorming for next year!

20........ ♥ WEEK 43

MONDAY
...... / ......

TUESDAY
...... / ......

WEDNESDAY
...... / ......

THURSDAY
...... / ......

FRIDAY
...... / ......

SATURDAY
...... / ......

SUNDAY
...... / ......

MONDAY
.... / ....

TUESDAY
.... / ....

WEDNESDAY
.... / ....

THURSDAY
.... / ....

FRIDAY
.... / ....

SATURDAY
.... / ....

SUNDAY
.... / ....

DRIP PAINT PUMPKIN CRAFT

Barbie and her sisters love this pumpkin craft because each one that you create will be totally unique! You can express your style by using a pumpkin in any size and paint it in your favorite colors.

WHAT YOU'LL NEED

- Large plastic garbage bag
- Pumpkin
- Latex based paints

INSTRUCTIONS

1. Place your pumpkin on the plastic garbage bag.
2. Slowly squeeze some paint at the top of the pumpkin, near the stem. Let the paint slowly drip down the sides of the pumpkin.
3. Repeat with a different color of paint, working around the entire pumpkin in as many colors and drips as you want!
4. Let the paint dry overnight while resting untouched on the plastic bag.

♥ WEEK 45   20 ....

MONDAY
.... / ....

TUESDAY
.... / ....

WEDNESDAY
.... / ....

THURSDAY
.... / ....

FRIDAY
.... / ....

SATURDAY
.... / ....

SUNDAY
.... / ....

Things That I'm Thankful for

Isn't Autumn just the best? Pumpkin-spiced drinks, cozy sweaters, and all those beautiful fall colors!
No wonder it's the season of gratitude!
There are just so many things to be thankful for.
Take some time to think about some of the things that you are thankful for and write them down here.

MONDAY

.... / ....

TUESDAY

.... / ....

WEDNESDAY

.... / ....

THURSDAY

.... / ....

FRIDAY

.... / ....

SATURDAY

.... / ....

SUNDAY

.... / ....

THANKSGIVING MEMORIES

We celebrated this Thanksgiving at

....

The people that I celebrated with were

....

....

....

Our Thanksgiving feast included

....

....

....

My favorite Thanksgiving food is

....

I helped out by

....

....

....

The weather was

♡ Cold   ♡ Windy
♡ Rainy   ♡ Calm
♡ Warm   ♡ Snowy

The funniest thing I heard this Thanksgiving was

....

....

A special memory that I made this Thanksgiving was

....

....

....

20........ ♥ WEEK 47

MONDAY
...... / ......

TUESDAY
...... / ......

WEDNESDAY
...... / ......

THURSDAY
...... / ......

FRIDAY
...... / ......

SATURDAY
...... / ......

SUNDAY
...... / ......

MONDAY
.... / ....

TUESDAY
.... / ....

WEDNESDAY
.... / ....

THURSDAY
.... / ....

FRIDAY
.... / ....

SATURDAY
.... / ....

SUNDAY
.... / ....

MONDAY

.... / ....

TUESDAY

.... / ....

WEDNESDAY

.... / ....

THURSDAY

.... / ....

FRIDAY

.... / ....

SATURDAY

.... / ....

SUNDAY

.... / ....

HOT CHOCOLATE

Nothing is better than a warm and toasty cup of hot chocolate on a cold winter's day. Teresa's recipe for **Cinnamon Hot Chocolate** is *scrumptious*. You'll be glad you gave it a try!

Makes enough for 2 cozy cups

WHAT YOU'LL NEED

- Small saucepan
- Whisk
- 2 cups milk
- 2 tablespoons honey
- 1 teaspoons cinnamon
- 1 teaspoon sugar
- 1 teaspoon brown sugar
- 1 teaspoon vanilla extract
- 7 ounces dark chocolate, broken into squares
- Marshmallows

THE STEPS

1. With the heat set to low, combine all ingredients in a small saucepan.
2. While heating, whisk ingredients together, stirring often.
3. After a few minutes, gently raise the temperature to medium high.
4. Remove just before the mixture comes to a boil.
5. Enjoy with marshmallows plopped on top!

♥ WEEK 50   20 ....

MONDAY
.... / ....

TUESDAY
.... / ....

WEDNESDAY
.... / ....

THURSDAY
.... / ....

FRIDAY
.... / ....

SATURDAY
.... / ....

SUNDAY
.... / ....

Holiday Gift Lip Balm

Are the short days and long nights of winter making you feel a bit stir crazy? This refreshingly minty and super hydrating peppermint lip balm makes a great holiday gift idea!

What You'll Need

- A microwavable bowl and spoon
- 1-2 drops peppermint essential oil
- ¼ cup coconut oil
- ⅛ teaspoon lipstick in your favorite color
- A small, sterilized container with lid

Directions

1. In the microwavable bowl, add the coconut oil, lipstick, and peppermint oil.
2. Microwave for 20 to 30 seconds.
3. Stir well with a spoon.
4. Carefully pour into the container.

MONDAY
.... / ....

TUESDAY
.... / ....

WEDNESDAY
.... / ....

THURSDAY
.... / ....

FRIDAY
.... / ....

SATURDAY
.... / ....

SUNDAY
.... / ....

A Year in Review

What an amazing year! You've had so many new experiences, made wonderful memories with your friends and family, and learned even more about yourself and your world. Write down some highlights, so that you'll NEVER forget what an epic year it was!

An important thing I learned about myself ....

A new food that I tried and loved this year ....

The best movie I saw this year ....

A new game that I discovered ....

A field trip that I will never forget ....

My bravest moment was when I ....

A new friend I made this year ....

A place that I visited for the first time ....

The thing that I am most proud of this year ....

My favorite holiday memory ....

The best book that I read this year ....

The best memory that I made with my friends ....

My biggest moment of the year..

❤ WEEK 52   20 ....

MONDAY
...... / ......

TUESDAY
...... / ......

WEDNESDAY
...... / ......

THURSDAY
...... / ......

FRIDAY
...... / ......

SATURDAY
...... / ......

SUNDAY
...... / ......

My notes

My notes

MY NOTES